HOT & SPICY COOKING

TIGER BOOKS INTERNATIONAL
LONDON

INTRODUCTION

Spices can be defined quite simply as the dried parts, be they seeds, bark or fruit, of certain aromatic plants that usually flourish in hot countries. Such as prosaic definition does little, however, to explain the way in which spices can be used to transform the simplest of ingredients into rare and delicious dishes. They are the touch of magic at the heart of so many time-honoured styles of cookery that range geographically from China, through Asia, the Middle East and North Africa to Mexico, via the Caribbean. In modern kitchens, spices can be used both to re-create authentic and exotic dishes from these traditional cuisines, and as a starting point for the creative cook to produce her own innovative dishes.

Historically, the primary use of spices was to disguise as much as to enhance, for ingredients were often far from fresh and people's diet was also bland and monotonous. Nowadays, we need only use spices to add their wonderful flavour, warmth and depth to dishes. The secondary use of spices was for their curative properties. It is only relatively recently that food and medicine have become as separate as they now are in most Western societies. When a link between them existed, spices were used not only for their effect on a person's taste buds but also for their effect on his health.

When buying spices, it is always preferable to buy whole ones wherever possible, and then to grind them as required. Whether whole or ready ground, spices should only ever be bought in small quantities, which can be used quickly, for the best and freshest flavour.

The thirty recipes brought together here are drawn from the many and varied cuisines that feature hot and spicy dishes in their repertoire, and they allow the creative cook to explore the whole range of tastes that cooking with spices opens up, from sizzling starters to exotic puddings.

3382
This edition published 1993 by Tiger Books International PLC, London
© 1993 CLB Publishing, Godalming, Surrey
Printed and bound in Singapore
All rights reserved
ISBN 1 85501 354 1

CURRY SOUP WITH MEATBALLS

A hearty soup which is perfect for heating up a cold winter night.

SERVES 4

Meatballs
225g/8oz lean minced beef
1 clove garlic, crushed
1 onion, peeled and finely chopped
½ tsp salt
½ tsp curry powder, or ¼ tsp curry paste
½ tsp ground cinnamon
½ tsp ground cloves
½ tsp ground pepper
30g/1oz breadcrumbs
1 small egg, lightly beaten

Peanut oil

Broth
1 tsp garam masala
1 tsp turmeric
1 onion, peeled and finely chopped
1 tsp curry leaves
570ml/1 pint water
1 clove garlic, crushed
½ cup desiccated coconut, soaked in 1 cup
   hot water for 15 minutes.

1. Mix together meatball ingredients, and form into small balls about the size of walnuts.

2. Heat wok, add oil and, when hot, fry meatballs. When browned well all over, remove with a slotted spoon, and drain on absorbent paper.

3. Carefully drain oil from wok. Add 1 tsp of oil, and fry spices for the broth for 30 seconds.

4. Add onion, curry leaves, and garlic, and cook together for 3 minutes.

5. Meanwhile, strain coconut in a sieve, press out as much liquid as possible, and discard the pulp.

6. Add water and coconut milk to the wok and simmer together for 5 minutes.

7. Adjust seasoning. Strain soup and return to wok. Add meatballs and simmer a further 5 minutes. Serve hot.

TIME: Preparation takes 30 minutes, cooking takes 20 minutes.

BUYING GUIDE: You will often find curry leaves in jars on the spice counter in supermarkets.

HOT AND SOUR SOUP

*A very warming soup, this is a favourite in winter in Peking. Add
chilli sauce and vinegar to suit your taste.*

SERVES 4–6

60g/2oz pork

3 dried Chinese mushrooms, soaked in
    boiling water for 5 minutes and chopped

60g/2oz peeled, uncooked prawns

1.5ltrs/2½ pints chicken stock

30g/1oz bamboo shoots, sliced

3 spring onions, shredded

Salt and pepper

1 tbsp sugar

1 tsp dark soy sauce

½ tsp light soy sauce

1-2 tsps chilli sauce

1½ tbsps vinegar

Dash sesame seed oil and rice wine or
    sherry

1 egg, well beaten

2 tbsps water mixed with 1 tbsp cornflour

---

1. Trim any fat from the pork and slice it
into shreds about 5cm/2 inches long and
less than 5mm/½-inch thick.

2. Soak the mushrooms in boiling water
until softened. Place the pork in a large pot
with the prawns and stock. Bring to the boil
and then reduce the heat to allow to
simmer gently for 4-5 minutes. Add all the
remaining ingredients except for the egg
and cornflour and water mixture. Cook a
further 1-2 minutes over low heat.

3. Remove the pan from the heat and add
the egg gradually, stirring gently until it
forms threads in the soup.

4. Mix a spoonful of the hot soup with the
cornflour and water mixture and add to the
soup, stirring constantly.

5. Bring the soup back to simmering point
for 1 minute to thicken the cornflour. Serve
immediately.

TIME: Preparation takes 25 minutes, cooking takes 7-8 minutes.

PREPARATION: Vary the amount of chilli sauce to suit your own taste.

VARIATION: Hot and Sour Soup is very versatile. Substitute other
ingredients such as chicken, crabmeat, bean sprouts, spinach or green
cabbage.

WATCHPOINT: The soup must be hot enough to cook the egg when it is
added, but not so hot that the egg sets immediately.

PRAWNS ACAPULCO

These make a stylish starter or a quickly prepared snack. Make the bread slices smaller to serve with cocktails.

SERVES 4

4 slices bread, crusts removed
90g/6 tbsps softened butter
175g/6oz cooked and peeled prawns
½ tsp chilli powder
¼ tsp paprika
¼ tsp cumin
Salt and pepper
Watercress to garnish

1. Cut the bread slices in half and spread with 30g/2 tbsps butter. Butter both sides sparingly.

2. Place the bread on a baking sheet and cook in a preheated 180°C/350°F/Gas Mark 4 oven for 10-15 minutes until golden brown. Keep warm.

3. Melt the remaining butter in a small pan and add the prawns, spices and seasoning and stir well.

4. Heat through completely and spoon on top of the bread slices. Garnish with watercress and serve hot.

TIME: Preparation takes 15 minutes, cooking 25 minutes.

WATCHPOINT: Do not heat the prawns too long or at too high a temperature; they toughen easily.

COOK'S TIP: The bread may be prepared in advance and reheated 5 minutes in the oven. Do not reheat the prawns.

CHICKEN TIKKA

Chicken Tikka is one of the most popular chicken dishes cooked in the Tandoor, the Indian clay oven. This recipe is adapted to cook the chicken in the conventional oven at a high temperature.

SERVES 4

450g/1lb boneless, skinned chicken breast

1 tsp salt

Juice of ½ a lemon

½ tsp tandoori colour or a few drops of red food colouring mixed with 1 tbsp tomato purée

2 cloves garlic, peeled and coarsely chopped

½-inch cube of root ginger, peeled and coarsely chopped

2 tsps ground coriander

½ tsp ground allspice or garam masala

¼ of a whole nutmeg, finely grated

½ tsp ground turmeric

125g/5oz thick set natural yogurt

4 tbsps corn or vegetable oil

½ tsp chilli powder

---

1. Cut the chicken into 1-inch cubes. Sprinkle with ½ tsp salt from the specified amount, and the lemon juice – mix thoroughly, cover and keep aside for 30 minutes.

2. Put the rest of the ingredients into an electric food processor or liquidiser and blend until smooth.

3. Put this marinade into a sieve and hold the sieve over the chicken pieces. Press the marinade through the sieve with the back of a metal spoon until only a very coarse mixture is left.

4. Coat the chicken thoroughly with the sieved marinade, cover the container and leave to marinate for 6-8 hours or overnight in the refrigerator.

5. Preheat the oven to 230°C/450°F/Gas Mark 8.

6. Line a roasting tin with aluminium foil (this will help to maintain the high level of temperature required to cook the chicken quickly without drying it out).

7. Thread the chicken onto skewers, leaving ¼-inch gap between each piece (this is necessary for the heat to reach all sides of the chicken).

8. Place the skewers in the prepared roasting tin and brush with some of the remaining marinade.

9. Cook in the centre of the oven for 6-8 minutes.

10. Take the tin out of the oven, turn the skewers over and brush the pieces of chicken with the remaining marinade.

11. Return the tin to the oven and cook for a further 6-8 minutes.

12. Shake off any excess liquid from the chicken.

13. Place the skewers on a serving dish. You may take the tikka off the skewers if you wish, but allow the meat to cool slightly before removing from the skewers.

TIME: Preparation takes 30–35 minutes plus time needed to marinate, cooking takes 15–18 minutes.

SPICED POTATO BITES

Boiled potatoes cut into small pieces and sautéed until they are brown and then flavoured with a light sprinkling of spices.

SERVES 6-8

675g/1½lbs potatoes
4 tbsps cooking oil
½ tbsp salt or to taste
¼ tsp garam masala
½ tsp ground cumin
½ tsp ground coriander
¼-½ tsp chilli powder

1. Boil the potatoes in their jacket, cool thoroughly, peel and dice them into 1-inch cubes.

2. In a wide shallow pan, preferably non-stick or cast iron, heat the oil over medium heat. It is important to have the right pan otherwise the potatoes will stick.

3. Add the potatoes and spread them evenly around the pan. Brown the potatoes evenly, stirring them occasionally.

4. When the potatoes are brown, sprinkle over the salt, garam masala, cumin, coriander and the chilli powder. Stir gently and mix until the potatoes are fully coated with the spices. Remove from the heat.

TIME: Preparation takes 30 minutes to boil the potatoes plus time to cool them, cooking takes 10-12 minutes.

SERVING IDEAS: Serve on cocktail sticks with drinks.

WATCHPOINT: The potatoes must be allowed to cool thoroughly. Hot or warm potatoes crumble easily and therefore cannot be cut into neat pieces.

SPAGHETTI AMATRICIANA

Red chilli pepper gives a kick to this easy pasta sauce.

SERVES 4

1 onion
6 strips smoked back bacon
450g/1lb ripe tomatoes
1 red chilli pepper
1½ tbsps oil
340g/12oz spaghetti

1. Slice the onion thinly. Remove rind from the bacon and cut into thin strips.

2. Drop the tomatoes into boiling water for 6-8 seconds. Remove with a draining spoon and place in cold water, and leave to cool completely. This will make the peels easier to remove.

3. When the tomatoes are peeled, cut them in half and remove the seeds and pulp with a teaspoon. Rub the seeds and pulp through a strainer and retain juice to use in the sauce if desired. Chop the tomato flesh roughly and set it aside.

4. Cut the stem off the chilli pepper and cut the pepper in half lengthways. Remove the seeds and core and cut the pepper into thin strips. Cut the strips into small dice.

5. Heat the oil in a sauté pan and add the onion and bacon. Stir over medium heat for about 5 minutes, until the onion is transparent. Drain off excess fat and add the tomatoes and chilli and mix well. Simmer the sauce gently, uncovered, for about 5 minutes, stirring occasionally.

6. Meanwhile, cook the spaghetti in boiling salted water with 1 tbsp oil for about 10-12 minutes. Drain and rinse in hot water and toss in a colander to dry. To serve, spoon the sauce on top of the spaghetti and sprinkle with freshly grated Parmesan cheese, if desired.

TIME: Spaghetti takes about 10-12 minutes to cook, sauce takes about 8 minutes to cook, preparation takes about 20-25 minutes.

COOK'S TIP: It is not necessary to use the whole chilli pepper; use as much as desired.

WATCHPOINT: Wash hands very well after handling chilli peppers or use rubber gloves while chopping them.

EGG AND POTATO DUM

Slow cooking, without any loss of steam, is the secret of the success of this Indian dish.

SERVES 4–6

6 hard-boiled eggs

5 tbsps cooking oil

450g/1lb medium-sized potatoes, peeled and quartered

⅛ tsp each of chilli powder and ground turmeric, mixed together

1 large onion, finely chopped

½-inch cube of root ginger, peeled and grated

1 cinnamon stick, 2-inches long; broken up into 2-3 pieces

2 black cardamoms, split open the top of each pod

4 whole cloves

1 fresh green chilli, chopped

1 small tin of tomatoes

½ tsp ground turmeric

2 tsps ground coriander

1 tsp ground fennel

¼-½ tsp chilli powder (optional)

1 tsp salt or to taste

225ml/8fl oz warm water

1 tbsp chopped coriander leaves

1. Shell the eggs and make 4 slits lengthwise on each egg leaving about ½-inch gap on either end.

2. Heat the oil over medium heat in a cast iron or non-stick pan (enamel or steel pans will cause the eggs and the potatoes to stick). Fry the potatoes until they are well browned on all sides (about 10 minutes). Remove them with a slotted spoon and keep aside.

3. Remove the pan from heat and stir in the turmeric and chilli mixture. Place the pan back on heat and fry the whole eggs until they are well browned. Remove them with a slotted spoon and keep aside.

4. In the same oil, fry the onions, ginger, cinnamon, cardamom, cloves and green chilli until the onions are lightly browned (6-7 minutes).

5. Add half the tomatoes, stir and fry until the tomatoes break up (2-3 minutes).

6. Add the turmeric, ground coriander, fennel and chilli powder (if used); stir and fry for 3-4 minutes.

7. Add the rest of the tomatoes and fry for 4-5 minutes, stirring frequently.

8. Add the potatoes, salt and water, bring to the boil, cover the pan tightly and simmer until the potatoes are tender, stirring occasionally.

9. Now add the eggs and simmer, uncovered for 5-6 minutes, stirring once or twice.

10. Stir in the coriander leaves and remove from heat.

TIME: Preparation takes 15 minutes, cooking takes 35-40 minutes.

SERVING IDEAS: Serve with Indian breads such as Puris or Loochis.

CHILLI PRAWN QUICHE

Fresh chilli peppers give a Mexican flavour to this quiche with its prawn filling.

SERVES 6

Pastry
100g/4oz plain flour
Pinch salt
2 tbsps butter or margarine
2 tbsps white cooking fat
2-4 tbsps cold water

Filling
4 eggs
140ml/¼ pint milk
140ml/¼ pint single cream
½ clove garlic, crushed
100g/4oz Cheddar cheese, grated
3 spring onions, chopped
2 green chillies, seeded and chopped
225g/8oz cooked and peeled prawns
Salt
Cooked, unpeeled prawns and parsley
    sprigs for garnish

1. Sift the flour with a pinch of salt into a mixing bowl, or place in a food processor and mix once or twice.

2. Rub in the butter and fat until the mixture resembles fine breadcrumbs, or work in the food processor, being careful not to over-mix.

3. Mix in the liquid gradually, adding enough to bring the pastry together into a ball. In a food processor, add the liquid through the funnel while the machine is running.

4. Wrap the pastry well and chill for 20-30 minutes.

5. Roll out the pastry on a well-floured surface with a floured rolling pin.

6. Wrap the circle of pastry around the rolling pin to lift it into a 25cm/10 inch flan dish. Unroll the pastry over the dish.

7. Carefully press the pastry onto the bottom and up the sides of the dish, taking care not to stretch it.

8. Roll the rolling pin over the top of the dish to remove excess pastry, or cut off with a sharp knife.

9. Mix the eggs, milk, cream and garlic together. Sprinkle the cheese, onion, chillies and prawns onto the base of the pastry and pour over the egg mixture.

10. Bake in a preheated 200°C/400°F/Gas Mark 6 oven for 30-40 minutes until firm and golden brown. Peel the tail shells off the prawns and remove the legs and roe if present. Use to garnish the quiche along with the sprigs of parsley.

TIME: Preparation takes about 40 minutes, which includes time for the pastry to chill. Cooking takes 30-40 minutes.

VARIATION: Add diced red or green peppers and chopped coriander leaves to the filling before baking.

SERVING IDEAS: Serve as a starter, cut in thin wedges or baked in individual dishes. Serve hot or cold with a salad for a snack or light meal.

SPICY EGG SALAD

*Serve this as a starter or a main course. If desired, substitute
more vegetables for the prawns.*

SERVES 4-6

4 eggs

Half a bunch of spring onions, chopped

Half a small red pepper, chopped

Half a small green pepper, chopped

100g/4oz cooked, peeled prawns

1 small jar artichoke hearts, drained and
    quartered

Dressing

90ml/6 tbsps oil

2 tbsps white wine vinegar

1 clove garlic, finely chopped

1 tsp dry mustard

½ tsp hot red pepper flakes

Salt

1. Prick the large end of the eggs with an
egg pricker or a needle.

2. Lower each egg carefully into boiling,
salted water. Bring the water back to the
boil, rolling the eggs in the water with the
bowl of a spoon.

3. Cook the eggs for 9 minutes once the
water comes back to the boil. Drain and
rinse under cold water until completely
cool. Peel and quarter. Combine the eggs
with the other ingredients in a large bowl.

4. Mix the dressing ingredients together
using a whisk to get a thick emulsion.

5. Pour the dressing over the salad and mix
carefully so that the eggs do not break up.

6. Serve on beds of shredded lettuce, if
desired.

TIME: Preparation takes about 25 minutes, cooking takes about 9 minutes
to boil the eggs.

PREPARATION: If preparing the eggs in advance, leave in the shells and in
cold water. This will prevent a grey ring forming around the yolks.

COOK'S TIP: Rolling the eggs around in the hot water helps to set the yolk
in the centre of the white and makes sliced or quartered eggs more
attractive.

PLAICE WITH SPICY TOMATO SAUCE

This piquant fish dish is popular along Mexico's Gulf coast.

SERVES 4

90g/3oz cream cheese
1 tsp dried oregano
Pinch cayenne pepper
4 whole fillets of plaice
Lime slices and dill to garnish

Tomato Sauce
1 tbsp oil
1 small onion, chopped
1 stick celery, chopped
1 chilli pepper, seeded and chopped
¼ tsp each ground cumin, coriander and
    ginger
½ red and ½ green pepper, seeded and
    chopped
400g/14oz canned tomatoes
1 tbsp tomato purée
Salt, pepper and a pinch sugar

1. Heat the oil in a heavy-based pan and cook the onion, celery, chilli pepper and spices for about 5 minutes over very low heat.

2. Add red and green peppers and the remaining ingredients and bring to the boil. Reduce heat and simmer 15-20 minutes, stirring occasionally. Set aside while preparing the fish.

3. Mix the cream cheese, oregano and cayenne pepper together and set aside.

4. Skin the fillets using a filleting knife. Start at the tail end and hold the knife at a slight angle to the skin.

5. Push the knife along using a sawing motion, with the blade against the skin. Dip fingers in salt to make it easier to hold onto the fish skin. Gradually separate the fish from the skin.

6. Spread the cheese filling on all 4 fillets and roll each up. Secure with cocktail sticks.

7. Place the fillets in a lightly greased baking dish, cover and cook for 10 minutes in a preheated 180°C/350°F/Gas Mark 4 oven.

8. Pour over the tomato sauce and cook a further 10-15 minutes. Fish is cooked when it feels firm and looks opaque. Garnish with lime slices and dill.

TIME: Preparation takes about 30 minutes, cooking takes 20-25 minutes.

SERVING IDEAS: Add rice and an avocado salad.

VARIATION: Add prawns or crabmeat to the filling for a dinner party dish.

SPICY FRIED FISH

The spice mixture used to coat the fish is very hot,
so use less if you want.

SERVES 4

4 fish fillets, about 225g/8oz each
225g/8oz unsalted butter
1 tbsp paprika
1 tsp garlic granules
1 tsp cayenne pepper
½ tsp ground white pepper
2 tsps salt
1 tsp dried thyme

1. Melt the butter and pour about half into each of four ramekin dishes and set aside.

2. Brush each fish fillet liberally with the remaining butter on both sides.

3. Mix together the spices and thyme and sprinkle generously on each side of the fillets, patting it on by hand.

4. Heat a large frying pan and add about 1 tbsp butter per fish fillet. When the butter is hot, add the fish, skin side down first.

5. Turn the fish over when the underside is very brown and repeat with the remaining side. Add more butter as necessary during cooking.

6. When the top side of the fish is very dark brown, repeat with the remaining fish fillets, keeping them warm while cooking the rest.

7. Serve the fish immediately with the dishes of butter for dipping.

TIME: Preparation takes about 20 minutes, cooking takes about 2 minutes per side for each fillet.

VARIATION: Use whatever varieties of fish fillets or steaks you like but make sure they are approximately 2cm/¾ inch thick.

PREPARATION: The fish should be very dark brown on the top and the bottom before serving. Leave at least 2 minutes before attempting to turn the fish over.

GRILLED FISH WITH ROMESCU

*Romescu is a sauce that evolved from a fish stew recipe and is still often
considered a dish on its own. It is simple to make and
has a strong, pungent taste.*

SERVES 4

900g/2lbs whole fish such as trout, red
    mullet, herring, sardines or mackerel,
    allowing 1-4 fish per person, depending
    on size
Bay leaves
Salt and pepper
Olive oil
Lemon juice

Romescu (Almond and Hot Pepper Sauce)
1 tomato, peeled, seeded and chopped
3 tbsps ground almonds
½ clove garlic, crushed
½ tsp cayenne pepper
Pinch salt
3 tbsps red wine vinegar
175ml/6 fl oz olive oil

1. To prepare the sauce, combine all the
ingredients, except the olive oil and
vinegar, in a mortar and pestle and work to
a smooth mixture.

2. Transfer to a bowl, whisk in red wine
vinegar and add the oil gradually, a few
drops at a time, mixing vigorously with a
wire whisk or a wooden spoon. Make sure
each addition of oil is absorbed before
adding more. Once about half the oil is
added, the remainder may be poured in in
a thin, steady stream. Adjust the seasoning
and set the sauce aside.

3. Wash the fish well, sprinkle the cavities
with salt and pepper and place in a bay
leaf. Brush the skin with olive oil and
sprinkle with lemon juice. Place under a
preheated grill and cook for about 2-5
minutes per side, depending on the
thickness of the fish. Brush with lemon
juice and olive oil while the fish is grilling.
Serve with the sauce and lemon or lime
wedges if desired.

TIME: Preparation takes about 20 minutes, cooking takes about 10-20
minutes.

PREPARATION: The sauce may be made several days in advance and stored
tightly sealed in the refrigerator. Allow the sauce to come to room
temperature and whisk again before serving.

SERVING IDEAS: Serve with boiled or fried potatoes and a salad.

PRAWN CHILLI MASALA

This is a delicate but richly flavoured Indian dish.

SERVES 4

90g/3oz unsalted butter

6 green cardamoms, split open the top of
    each pod

1-inch cube of root ginger, peeled and
    finely grated

3-4 cloves garlic, peeled and crushed

1 tbsp ground coriander

½ tsp ground turmeric

450g/1lb fresh peeled prawns

125g/5oz thick set natural yogurt

90ml/3fl oz water

1 tsp sugar

1 tsp salt or to taste

30g/1oz ground almonds

4-6 whole fresh green chillies

2 fresh green chillies, seeded and minced

½ tsp garam masala

1 tbsp chopped coriander leaves

1. Melt 60g/2oz butter from the specified amount over gentle heat and add the whole cardamoms, fry for 30 seconds and add the ginger and garlic. Stir and cook for 1 minute, then add the ground coriander and turmeric. Stir and fry for 30 seconds.

2. Add the prawns, turn the heat up to medium and cook for 5-6 minutes, stirring frequently.

3. Beat the yogurt until smooth, gradually add the water and beat until well blended. Add this mixture to the prawns, stir in the sugar and the salt, cover the pan and simmer for 5-6 minutes.

4. Add the ground almonds and the whole green chillies and cook, uncovered, for 5 minutes.

5. Meanwhile, fry the onions in the remaining 30g/1oz butter until they are just soft, but not brown. Add the minced green chillies and the garam masala; stir and fry for a further 1-2 minutes. Stir this mixture into the prawns along with any butter left in the pan. Remove the pan from the heat.

6. Put the prawns in a serving dish and garnish with the coriander leaves.

TIME: Preparation takes 15 minutes, cooking takes 20-25 minutes.

SERVING IDEAS: Serve with a Mushroom Pilau or Fried Brown Rice.

TO FREEZE: Suitable for freezing if fresh prawns are used.

SPICY SPANISH CHICKEN

Chilli peppers, coriander and sunny tomatoes add a warm Spanish flavour to grilled chicken.

SERVES 6

6 boned chicken breasts

Grated rind and juice of 1 lime

2 tbsps olive oil

Coarsely ground black pepper

90ml/6 tbsps whole grain mustard

2 tsps paprika

4 ripe tomatoes, peeled, seeded and
    quartered

2 shallots, chopped

1 clove garlic, crushed

½ Jalapeno pepper or other chilli, seeded
    and chopped

1 tsp wine vinegar

Pinch salt

2 tbsps chopped fresh coriander

Whole coriander leaves to garnish

1. Place chicken breasts in a shallow dish with the lime rind and juice, oil, pepper, mustard and paprika. Marinate for about 1 hour, turning occasionally.

2. To peel tomatoes easily, drop them into boiling water for about 5 seconds or less depending on ripeness. Place immediately in cold water. Peels should come off easily.

3. Place tomatoes, shallots, garlic, chilli pepper, vinegar and salt in a food processor or blender and process until coarsely chopped. Stir in the chopped coriander by hand.

4. Place chicken on a grill pan and reserve the marinade. Cook chicken skin side uppermost for about 7-10 minutes, depending on how close the chicken is to the heat source. Baste frequently with the remaining marinade. Grill other side in the same way. Sprinkle with salt after grilling.

5. Place chicken on serving plates and garnish top with coriander leaves or sprigs. Serve with a spoonful of the tomato relish on one side.

TIME: Preparation takes about 1 hour, cooking takes 14-20 minutes.

PREPARATION: Tomato relish can be prepared in advance and kept in the refrigerator. It can also be served with other poultry, meat or seafood. It also makes a good dip for vegetable crudités or tortilla chips.

WATCHPOINT: When preparing chilli peppers, wear rubber gloves – or at least be sure to wash hands thoroughly after handling them. Do not touch eyes or face before washing hands.

31

CHICKEN IN HOT PEPPER SAUCE

Stir-fried chicken served with peppers in a hot sauce.

SERVES 4

1 chicken
2 tbsps oil
1 tsp chopped garlic
1 green pepper, seeded and cut into thin
    strips
1 red pepper, seeded and cut into thin
    strips
1 tsp wine vinegar
1 tbsp light soy sauce
1 tsp sugar
340ml/12 fl oz chicken stock
1 tbsp chilli sauce
Salt and pepper

1. First, bone the chicken. To bone the legs, cut down along the bone on all sides, drawing out the bone with an even movement. Cut all the chicken meat into thin strips.

2. Heat the oil in a wok and stir-fry the garlic, chicken and the green and red peppers.

3. Pour off any excess oil and deglaze the wok with the vinegar. Stir in the soy sauce, sugar and stock.

4. Gradually stir in the chilli sauce, tasting after each addition. Season with a little salt and pepper to taste.

5. Cook until the sauce has reduced slightly. Serve piping hot.

TIME: Preparation takes 10 minutes, cooking takes approximately
25 minutes.

CHICKEN KORMA

The recipe below, though simple and prepared with readily available ingredients, has all the characteristic features of this classic north Indian dish.

SERVES 4-6

1.4kg/2½lbs chicken joints, skin removed

1-inch cube of root ginger, finely grated

125g/5oz thick set natural yogurt

1 small onion, coarsely chopped

3-4 dried red chillies

2-4 cloves garlic, peeled and coarsely chopped

5 tbsps cooking oil plus 2 tbsps extra oil

450g/1lb onions, finely sliced

1 tbsp ground coriander

½ tsp powdered black pepper

1 tsp garam masala

1 tsp ground turmeric

225ml/8fl oz warm water (reduce quantity if using boneless chicken)

90g/3oz creamed coconut, cut into small pieces

1¼ tsps salt or to taste

2 heaped tbsps ground almonds

Juice of ½ a lemon

---

1. Cut each chicken joint into half, separating leg from thigh and cutting each breast into two.

2. Mix with ginger and yogurt, cover and leave to marinate in a cool place for 2-4 hours or in the refrigerator overnight.

3. Place the chopped onion, red chillies and garlic in a liquidiser or food processor and liquidise to a smooth paste. You may need to add a little water if you are using a liquidiser.

4. Heat the 5 tbsps oil over medium heat and fry the sliced onions till they are golden brown. Remove the pan from the heat and using a slotted spoon, transfer the onions to another dish. Leave any remaining oil in the pan.

5. Place the pan in which the onions have been fried, over medium heat and add the other 2 tbsps cooking oil.

6. When hot, add the ground coriander, powdered pepper, garam masala and turmeric, stir rapidly (take the pan off the heat if the oil is too hot) and add the chicken along with the marinade. Adjust the heat to medium-high and fry the chicken for about 10 minutes, stirring frequently.

7. Add the liquidised spices and continue to fry for 6-8 minutes on low heat.

8. Add the water and the coconut and bring to the boil. Stir until coconut is dissolved. Add fried onion slices and salt.

9. Reduce heat to low, cover the pan and simmer until the chicken is tender (25-30 minutes). Sprinkle the ground almonds and mix well. Remove from heat and add the lemon juice.

TIME: Preparation takes 15 minutes plus time needed to marinate, cooking takes 55 minutes.

SERVING IDEAS: Serve with a Pilau Rice or Mushroom Pilau.

CORIANDER CHICKEN

Coriander Chicken is quick and easy to make, it tastes wonderful and looks very impressive – a perfect choice for any dinner party menu.

SERVES 4-6

1kg/2¼lbs chicken joints, skinned
2-4 cloves garlic, peeled and crushed
125g/5oz thick set natural yogurt
5 tbsps cooking oil
1 large onion, finely sliced
2 tbsps ground coriander
½ tsp ground black pepper
1 tsp ground mixed spice
½ tsp ground turmeric
½ tsp cayenne pepper or chilli powder
125ml/4fl oz warm water
1 tsp salt or to taste
30g/1oz ground almonds
2 hard-boiled eggs, sliced
¼ tsp paprika

1. Cut each chicken joint into two, mix thoroughly with the crushed garlic and the yogurt. Cover the container and leave to marinate in a cool place for 2-4 hours or overnight in the refrigerator.

2. Heat the oil over medium heat and fry the onions until they are golden brown (6-8 minutes). Remove with a slotted spoon and keep aside.

3. In the same oil, fry the coriander, ground pepper, ground mixed spice and turmeric for 15 seconds and add the chicken along with all the marinade in the container.

4. Adjust heat to medium-high and fry the chicken until it changes colour (5-6 minutes).

5. Add the cayenne or chilli powder, water, salt, and the fried onion slices. Bring to the boil, cover the pan and simmer until the chicken is tender (about 30 minutes).

6. Stir in the ground almonds and remove from heat. Garnish with slices of hard-boiled egg and a sprinkling of paprika.

TIME: Preparation takes 20 minutes plus time needed for marinating, cooking takes 45–50 minutes.

SERVING IDEAS: Serve with boiled rice or Pilau Rice.

WATCHPOINT: Reduce cooking time if boneless chicken is used.

SPICED BEEF

A classic recipe which requires the best-quality beef.

SERVES 2-3

Marinade

1 tsp sugar

2-3 star anise, ground

½ tsp ground fennel

1 tbsp dark soy sauce

¼ tsp monosodium glutamate (optional)

450g/1lb fillet of beef, cut into 2.5cm/1-inch strips

1-inch fresh root ginger, peeled and crushed

½ tsp salt

2 tbsps oil

4 spring onions, sliced

½ tsp freshly ground black pepper

1 tbsp light soy sauce

1. Mix the marinade ingredients together.

2. Add the beef strips, ginger and salt, and marinate for 20 minutes.

3. Heat the oil in wok and stir-fry the onions for 1 minute.

4. Add the beef, ground pepper and soy sauce and stir-fry for 4-5 minutes.

TIME: Preparation takes 30 minutes, cooking takes 5–6 minutes.

COOK'S TIP: Fresh root ginger keeps well if wrapped in food wrap and stored in the refrigerator.

CHILLI BEEF STEW

Beef, red onions, red peppers, paprika, tomatoes and red beans all go into this zesty stew.

SERVES 6–8

900g/2lbs beef chuck, cut into 2.5cm/1-inch pieces
Oil
1 large red onion, coarsely chopped
2 cloves garlic, crushed
2 red peppers, seeded and cut into 2.5cm/1-inch pieces
1-2 red chillies, seeded and finely chopped
3 tbsps mild chilli powder
1 tbsp cumin
1 tbsp paprika
850ml/1½ pints beer, water or stock
225g/8oz canned tomatoes, puréed
2 tbsps tomato purée
225g/8oz canned red kidney beans, drained
Pinch salt
6 ripe tomatoes, peeled, seeded and diced

1. Pour about 60ml/4 tbsps oil into a large saucepan or flameproof casserole. When hot, brown the meat in small batches over moderately high heat for about 5 minutes per batch.

2. Set aside the meat on a plate or in the lid of the casserole. Lower the heat and cook the onion, garlic, red peppers and chillies for about 5 minutes. Add the chilli powder, cumin and paprika and cook for 1 minute further. Pour on the liquid and add the canned tomatoes, tomato purée and the meat.

3. Cook slowly for about 1½-2 hours. Add the beans about 45 minutes before the end of cooking time.

4. When the meat is completely tender, add salt to taste and serve garnished with the diced tomatoes.

TIME: Preparation takes about 25 minutes, cooking takes about 1½-2 hours.

COOK'S TIP: The chilli may be frozen for up to 3 months in a tightly covered freezer container. Allow the chilli to cool completely before sealing and freezing. Defrost in the refrigerator and bring slowly to the boil before serving.

VARIATION: The chilli may be made with pork shoulder, with a mixture of beef and pork or minced beef or pork.

MEAT VINDALOO

Vindaloo is traditionally a hot curry, but the quantity of chillies can be adjusted to suit individual taste.

SERVES 4-6

Grind the following 5 ingredients in a coffee grinder

2 tbsps coriander seeds

1 tbsp cumin seeds

6-8 dried red chillies

1 tbsp mustard seeds

½ tsp fenugreek seeds

3-4 tbsps cider or white wine vinegar

1 tsp ground turmeric

1-inch cube of root ginger, peeled and finely grated

3-4 cloves garlic, peeled and crushed

1kg/2¼lbs shoulder of lamb or stewing steak

4 tbsps cooking oil

1 large onion, finely chopped

1-2 tsps chilli powder

1 tsp paprika

1¼ tsps salt or to taste

450ml/15fl oz warm water

2-3 medium-sized potatoes

1 tbsp chopped coriander leaves, (optional)

1. In a large bowl, make a thick paste out of the ground spices, by adding the vinegar.

2. Add the turmeric, ginger and garlic. Mix thoroughly.

3. Trim off excess fat from the meat and cut into 2.5cm/1-inch cubes.

4. Add the meat and mix it well so that all the pieces are fully coated with the paste. Cover the bowl with cling film and leave to marinate for 4-6 hours or overnight in the refrigerator.

5. Put the meat in a pan and place this over medium heat, allow the meat to heat through, stirring occasionally; this will take about 5 minutes. Cover the pan, and cook the meat in its own juice for 15-20 minutes or until the liquid is reduced to a thick paste. Stir occasionally during this time to ensure that the meat does not stick to the bottom of the pan. Remove from heat and keep aside.

6. Heat the oil over medium heat and fry the onions until they are soft (about 5 minutes).

7. Add the meat and fry for 6-8 minutes stirring frequently.

8. Add the chilli powder, paprika and salt. Stir and fry for a further 2-3 minutes.

9. Add the water, bring to the boil, cover and simmer for 40-45 minutes or until the meat is nearly tender (beef will take longer to cook, check water level and add more water if necessary).

10. Meanwhile, peel and wash the potatoes. Cut them into approximately 3cm/1½-inch cubes. Add this to the meat and bring to the boil again. Cover the pan and simmer until the potatoes are cooked (15-20 minutes).

11. Turn the vindaloo on to a serving dish and sprinkle the coriander leaves on top.

TIME: Preparation takes 10-15 minutes plus time needed for marinating, cooking takes 1 hour 15 minutes.

LEG OF LAMB WITH CHILLI SAUCE

Give Sunday roast lamb a completely different taste with a spicy orange sauce.

SERVES 4

1kg/2¼lbs leg of lamb

Marinade
1 tsp cocoa powder
¼ tsp cayenne pepper
½ tsp ground cumin
½ tsp paprika
½ tsp ground oregano
¼ pint water
¼ pint orange juice
¼ pint red wine
1 clove of garlic, crushed
2 tbsps brown sugar
1 tbsp cornflour
Pinch salt
Orange slices and coriander to garnish

1. If the lamb has a lot of surface fat, trim slightly with a sharp knife. If possible, remove the paper-thin skin on the outside of the lamb. Place lamb in a shallow dish.

2. Mix together the marinade ingredients, except cornflour, and pour over the lamb, turning it well to coat completely. Cover and refrigerate for 12-24 hours, turning occasionally.

3. Drain the lamb, reserving the marinade, and place in a roasting pan. Cook in a preheated 180°C/350°F/Gas Mark 4 oven for about 2 hours until meat is cooked according to taste.

4. Baste occasionally with the marinade and pan juices.

5. Remove lamb to a serving dish and keep warm. Skim the fat from the top of the roasting pan with a large spoon and discard.

6. Pour remaining marinade into the pan juices in the roasting pan and bring to the boil, stirring to loosen the sediment. Mix cornflour with a small amount of water and add some of the liquid from the roasting pan. Gradually stir cornflour mixture into the pan and bring back to the boil.

7. Cook, stirring constantly, until thickened and clear. Add more orange juice, wine or water as necessary.

8. Garnish the lamb with orange slices and sprigs of coriander. Pour over some of the sauce and serve the rest separately.

TIME: Preparation takes about 15 minutes, with 12–24 hours for the lamb to marinate. Cooking takes about 2 hours for the lamb and 20 minutes to finish the sauce.

VARIATION: The marinade ingredients can also be used with beef or poultry.

SERVING IDEAS: Serve with rice or boiled potatoes and vegetables.

KOFTA (MEATBALL) CURRY

*Koftas are popular throughout India, and they are made using fine lean mince
which is blended with herbs and spices.*

SERVES 4

For the koftas

450g/1lb lean minced lamb
2 cloves garlic, peeled and chopped
½-inch cube of root ginger, peeled and
    coarsely chopped
1 small onion, coarsely chopped
60ml/2fl oz water
1 fresh green chilli, seeded and chopped
2 tbsps chopped coriander leaves
1 tbsp fresh mint leaves, chopped
1 tsp salt or to taste

For the gravy

5 tbsps cooking oil
2 medium-sized onions, finely chopped
½-inch cube of root ginger, peeled and
    grated
2 cloves garlic, peeled and crushed
2 tsps ground coriander
1½ tsps ground cumin
½ tsp ground turmeric
¼-½ tsp chilli powder
1 small tin of tomatoes
150ml/5fl oz warm water
½ tsp salt or to taste
2 black cardamom pods, opened
4 whole cloves
2-inch piece of cinnamon stick, broken up
2 bay leaves, crumpled
2 tbsps thick set natural yogurt
2 tbsps ground almonds
1 tbsp chopped coriander leaves

1. Put half the mince, all the garlic, ginger,
onion and the water into a saucepan and
place over medium heat. Stir until the mince
is heated through.

2. Cover and simmer until all liquid
evaporates (30-35 minutes) then cook
uncovered if necessary, to dry out excess
liquid.

3. Combine the cooked mince with the rest of
the ingredients, including the raw mince.

4. Put the mixture into a food processor or
liquidiser and blend until smooth. Chill the
mixture for 30 minutes.

5. Divide the mixture into approximately 20
balls, each slightly bigger than a walnut.

6. Rotate each ball between your palms to
make neat round koftas.

7. Heat the oil over medium heat and fry the
onions until they are just soft.

8. Add the ginger and garlic and fry for 1
minute.

9. Add the coriander, cumin, turmeric and
chilli powder and stir quickly.

10. Add one tomato at a time, along with a
little juice to the spice mixture, stirring until
mixture begins to look dry.

11. Now add the water, salt, cardamom,
cloves, cinnamon and the bay leaves.

12. Stir once and add the koftas. Bring to the
boil, cover and simmer for 5 minutes.

13. Beat the yogurt with a fork until smooth,
add the ground almonds and beat again – stir
GENTLY into the curry. Cover and simmer
until the koftas are firm.

14. Stir the curry GENTLY, cover again, and
simmer for a further 10–15 minutes, stirring
occasionally to ensure that the thickened
gravy does not stick to the pan.

15. Stir in the coriander leaves and remove
from heat.

SPICY MEAT PIES

These meat pies are fried rather than baked. Add cayenne gradually to taste.

MAKES 8

Pastry

3 tbsps butter or margarine

2 eggs

60-90ml/4-6 tbsps milk or water

300-400g/10-14oz plain flour

Pinch sugar and salt

Filling

2 tbsps butter or margarine

½ small onion, finely chopped

½ small green pepper, finely chopped

1 stick celery, finely chopped

1 clove garlic, crushed

340g/12oz minced pork

1 bay leaf, finely crushed

1 tsp cayenne pepper

Pinch salt

2 tbsps flour

280ml/½ pint beef stock

1 tbsp tomato purée

1 tsp dried thyme

1. To prepare the pastry, soften the butter or margarine in a food processor or with an electric mixer until creamy. Beat in the eggs one at a time and add the milk or water.

2. Sift in 300g/10oz flour, sugar and salt and mix until blended. If necessary, add the remaining flour gradually until the mixture forms a ball. Wrap well and refrigerate about 30 minutes.

3. Melt the butter or margarine in a large frying pan and cook the onion, pepper, celery, garlic and pork over moderate heat. Break up the meat with a fork as it cooks.

4. Add the bay leaf, cayenne pepper, salt and flour and cook, scraping the bottom of the pan often, until the flour browns.

5. Pour on the stock and stir in the tomato purée and thyme. Bring to the boil and cook, stirring occasionally, until thickened. Chill thoroughly and remove the bay leaf.

6. Divide the pastry into 8 pieces and roll each out to a circle about 3mm/⅛ inch thick.

7. Spread the chilled filling on half of each circle to within 1.25cm/½ inch of the edge. Brush the edge with water.

8. Fold over and seal the edges together firmly. Crimp the edges with a fork.

9. Heat oil in a deep sauté pan or a deep fat fryer to about 180°C/350°F. Fry 2 or 3 pies at a time for about 2 minutes, holding them under the surface of the oil with a metal spoon to brown evenly. Remove from the oil with a draining spoon and drain on paper towels. Serve immediately.

TIME: Preparation takes about 30-40 minutes, cooking takes about 15 minutes for the filling and 2 minutes for each batch of 2 pies.

COOK'S TIP: The dough may be prepared in advance and kept in a refrigerator for about 2 days.

VARIATION: Minced beef may be substituted for the pork. Double the quantity of vegetables for a vegetarian filling.

SPICY RICE AND BEAN PILAFF

A lively side dish or vegetarian main course, this recipe readily takes to creative variations and makes a good cold salad.

SERVES 6-8

60ml/4 tbsps oil
225g/8oz long grain rice
1 onion, finely chopped
1 green pepper, seeded and chopped
1 tsp each ground cumin and coriander
Dash tabasco sauce
Salt
1 litre/1¾ pints vegetable stock
450g/1lb canned red kidney beans, drained and rinsed
450g/1lb canned tomatoes, drained and coarsely chopped
Chopped parsley

1. Heat the oil in a casserole or a large, deep saucepan.

2. Add the rice and cook until just turning opaque. Add the onion, pepper and cumin and coriander. Cook gently for a further 2 minutes.

3. Add the tabasco, salt, stock and beans and bring to the boil. Cover and cook about 45 minutes, or until the rice is tender and most of the liquid is absorbed.

4. Remove from the heat and add the tomatoes, stirring them in gently. Leave to stand, covered, for 5 minutes.

5. Fluff up the mixture with a fork and sprinkle with parsley to serve.

TIME: Preparation takes about 25 minutes, cooking takes about 50 minutes.

SERVING IDEAS: Serve with bread and a salad for a light vegetarian meal. Serve as a side dish with meat or poultry, or cheese and egg dishes.

VARIATION: The recipe may be made with 450g/1lb fresh tomatoes, peeled, seeded and coarsely chopped.

CHANA MASALA

*An excellent dish to serve hot as a main course or cold
as an accompaniment to a nut loaf.*

SERVES 4

1 large onion, chopped

4 cloves garlic, crushed

¾-inch fresh ginger, peeled and finely
    chopped

3 tbsps ghee

1 tbsp ground coriander

2 tsps cumin seed

¼ tsp cayenne pepper

1 tsp turmeric

2 tsps roasted cumin seed, ground

1 tbsp amchur (dried mango powder) or
    1 tbsp lemon juice

2 tsps paprika

400g/1 × 14oz tin Italian tomatoes

675g/1½lbs cooked chickpeas
    (12oz uncooked)

1 tsp garam masala

½ tsp salt

1 fresh green chilli, finely chopped

1. Sauté the onion, garlic and ginger in the ghee until soft.

2. Add all the spices and fry over a low heat for 1-2 minutes stirring all the time.

3. Add the tomatoes, roughly chopped, together with their juice.

4. Add the cooked chickpeas.

5. Cook for 30 minutes over a medium heat.

6. Add the garam masala, salt and chilli, stir well and serve.

TIME: Preparation takes about 15 minutes, cooking takes 30 minutes.

WATCHPOINT: Fry the spices over a low heat to ensure they do not burn.

VARIATION: Small pieces of diced vegetables such as potatoes, fresh tomatoes or cauliflower may be added.

SPICED GREEN BEANS

Sliced green beans braised with a few spices, then tossed in roasted, ground sesame seeds, create the unique flavour of this dish.

SERVES 4-6

2 tbsps sesame seeds

3 tbsps cooking oil

¼ tsp black mustard seeds

4-6 cloves garlic, peeled and finely chopped

1-2 dried red chillies, coarsely chopped

½ tsp ground turmeric

1 tsp ground coriander

450g/1lb frozen sliced green beans, defrosted and drained

¾ tsp salt or to taste

1 tbsp desiccated coconut

1. Heat an iron griddle or other heavy-based pan over medium heat and dry-roast the sesame seeds until they are lightly browned, stirring constantly. Transfer them to a plate and allow to cool.

2. Heat the oil over medium heat and add the mustard seeds. When they begin to pop, add the garlic and allow it to turn slightly brown.

3. Add the red chillies, turmeric and coriander, stir briskly and add the beans and salt. Mix thoroughly, lower heat to minimum setting, cover the pan tightly and cook until the beans are tender (15-20 minutes), stirring occasionally.

4. Grind the sesame seeds and the coconut in a coffee grinder and stir into the beans. Remove the pan from the heat.

TIME: Preparation takes 10-15 minutes, cooking takes 25-30 minutes.

SERVING IDEAS: Serve with spicy meat and poultry dishes.

TARKA DHAL (SPICED LENTILS)

Dhal of some sort is always cooked as part of a meal in an Indian household.
As a vast majority of the Indian population is vegetarian, dhal is a good
source of protein.

SERVES 4

175g/6oz Masoor dhal (red split lentils)
700ml/1¼ pint water
1 tsp ground turmeric
1 tsp ground cumin
1 tsp salt or to taste
30g/1oz ghee or unsalted butter
1 medium-sized onion, finely chopped
2 cloves garlic, peeled and finely chopped
2 dried red chillies, coarsely chopped

1. Put the dhal, water, turmeric, cumin and salt into a saucepan and bring the liquid to the boil.

2. Reduce heat to medium and cook uncovered for 8-10 minutes, stirring frequently.

3. Now cover the pan and simmer for 30 minutes, stirring occasionally.

4. Remove the dhal from the heat, allow to cool slightly and mash through a sieve.

5. Melt the ghee or butter over medium heat and fry the onion, garlic and red chillies until the onions are well browned (8-10 minutes).

6. Stir in half the fried onion mixture to the dhal and put the dhal in a serving dish. Arrange the remaining fried onions on top.

TIME: Preparation takes about 10 minutes, cooking takes about 50 minutes.

SERVING IDEAS: Serve with Plain Boiled Rice.

WATCHPOINT: Pulses tend to froth and spill over. The initial cooking without the lid in stage 2 should help to eliminate this problem, but should you find that it is spilling over, then partially cover the pan until the froth settles down; this should take only a few minutes.

MANGO DELIGHT

Fresh, ripe mangoes are superb for this dessert. After slicing them, gently scrape off every bit of flesh next to the stones. Though they will not be in neat pieces, they will add a lot to the flavour when mixed with the custard-cream base used for this dish.

SERVES 4-6

2 fresh ripe mangoes or 2 × 425g/15oz tins of sliced mangoes
2 tbsps custard powder
2 tbsps sugar
150ml/5fl oz milk
1 tsp ground cardamom or ground mixed spice
150ml/5fl oz double cream
2 tbsps shelled unsalted pistachio nuts, lightly crushed

1. Drain one tin of the mango slices and purée them in an electric liquidiser or food processor. Now drain the other can and coarsely chop the mango slices. Peel, slice and chop fresh mangoes.

2. Mix custard powder and sugar together, gradually add the milk and blend well. Cook over low heat until the consistency resembles whipped cream.

3. Stir in the ground cardamom or mixed spice and remove from heat.

4. Gradually add the mango pulp to the custard mix, stirring all the time.

5. Whisk the cream until fairly thick, but still pouring consistency. If you buy extra thick double cream, there is no need to whisk it.

6. Stir the cream into the mango mixture and gently mix in the chopped mangoes.

7. Transfer the mango mixture into a serving bowl and top with the crushed pistachio nuts. Serve hot or cold.

TIME: Preparation takes 10 minutes, cooking takes 10 minutes.

SPICED FRUIT SALAD

Exotic fruits served with a richly flavoured syrup.

SERVES 6-8

425g/15oz tin pineapple chunks
425g/15oz tin papaya (paw paw) chunks
425g/15oz tin mango slices, cut into chunks
425g/15oz tin guava halves, cut into chunks
3 cinnamon sticks, each 2-inches long
3 black cardamoms
6 whole cloves
8 black peppercorns

1. Drain all the fruits and reserve the syrup. Mix all the syrup together, reserve 570ml/20fl oz and drain off remainder.

2. Put the syrup into a saucepan and add the spices, bring to the boil, cover the pan and let it simmer for 20 minutes.

3. Uncover and reduce the syrup to half its original volume by boiling for 5-6 minutes. Remove from heat and allow the syrup to cool.

4. Keep the pan covered until the syrup cools, (in an open pan some of the flavour will be lost).

5. Reserve a few pieces of papaya and guava and all the mangoes. Arrange the remaining fruits in a serving bowl.

6. Arrange the mangoes on top, then put in the reserved papaya and guava.

7. Strain the spiced syrup and pour over the fruits. Cover with cling film and chill.

TIME: Preparation takes 10-15 minutes, cooking takes 20 minutes.

VARIATION: Use fresh ripe William pear instead of tinned mango.
Add 1 tbsp of brandy to the syrup.

CARAMEL CUSTARD WITH ORANGE AND CORIANDER

This is one of the best loved puddings in Spain. Fragrant coriander gives it new appeal and its flavour is marvellous with orange.

SERVES 8

175g/6oz sugar
90ml/6 tbsps water
3 small oranges
850ml/1½ pints milk
1 tbsp coriander seeds, crushed
6 eggs
2 egg yolks
175g/6oz sugar

1. To prepare the caramel, put the sugar and water in a heavy-based saucepan and bring to the boil over gentle heat to dissolve the sugar.

2. Once the sugar is dissolved, bring to the boil over high heat and cook to a golden brown, watching the colour carefully.

3. While the caramel is cooking, heat 8 ramekin dishes to warm them. When the caramel is brown, pour an equal amount into each dish and swirl the dish quickly to coat the base and sides with caramel. Leave the caramel to cool and harden in the dishes.

4. Grate the oranges and combine the rind, milk and crushed coriander seeds in a deep saucepan. Set the oranges aside for later use. Bring the milk almost to the boiling point and set it aside for the flavours to infuse.

5. Beat the eggs, yolks and sugar together until light and fluffy. Gradually strain on the milk, stirring well in between each addition. Pour the milk over the caramel in each dish. Place the dishes in a bain-marie and place in a preheated 170°C/325°F/Gas Mark 3 oven for about 40 minutes, or until a knife inserted into the centre of the custards comes out clean. Lower the oven temperature slightly if the water begins to boil around the dishes.

6. When the custards are cooked, remove the dishes from the bain-marie and refrigerate for at least 3 hours or overnight until the custard is completely cold and set.

7. To serve, loosen the custards from the sides of the dish with a small knife and turn them out onto individual plates. Peel the white pith from around the oranges and segment them. Place some of the orange segments around the custards and serve immediately.

TIME: Preparation takes about 30-40 minutes, cooking time for the custards is about 40 minutes.

WATCHPOINT: The sugar and water can burn easily once it comes to the boil, so watch it carefully.

PREPARATION: A bain-marie literally means a water bath. To make one, pour warm water into a roasting pan, the level to come half way up the sides of the dish or dishes being used. This protects delicate egg custard mixtures from the direct heat of the oven. Check from time to time to see that the water is not boiling.

INDEX